HISTORY
MYSTERIES REVEALED

Natalie Hyde

Author: Natalie Hyde

Editor: Molly Aloian

Proofreader: Crystal Sikkens

Project coordinator: Kathy Middleton

Production coordinator: Katherine Berti

Prepress technician: Katherine Berti

Project editor: Tom Jackson

Designer: Paul Myerscough, Calcium Creative

Picture researcher: Clare Newman

Managing editor: Tim Harris

Art director: Jeni Child

Design manager: David Poole

Editorial director: Lindsey Lowe

Children's publisher: Anne O'Daly

Photographs:
Alamy: North Wind Picture Archives: p. 29 (top)
Bridgeman Art Library: p. 29 (bottom)
Corbis: Atlantide Phototravel: p. 9 (top); Bettmann:
    p. 26, Richard A. Cooke: p. 28; Hugh Sitton:
    p. 27; Staffan Widstrand: p. 7
Istockphoto: Joseph Luoman: p. 11 (top); Milan
    Systemtecnik: p. 8 (top); Klaus Nilkens:
    p. 10 (bottom)
JI Unlimited: p. 19, 21 (top and bottom)
Library of Congress: p. 15, 22 (bottom)
Press Association Images: p. 17 (top)
Robert Hunt Library: p. 23
Shutterstock: George Bailey: p. 1; Tyler Bayes: p. 30;
    Bryan Busovicki: p. 16 (top); Elias H. Debbas II:
    p. 25 (bottom left); Elena Elisseeva: p. 11 (bottom);
    Vladislav Gurfunkel: p. 18 (bottom); IPK Photography:
    p. 7 (top right); Javarman: p. 16 (bottom); Igor
    Kisselev: p. 22 (top); Kmirgaya: p. 8 (bottom);
    Litvan Leonid: p. 20; Pete Niesen: p. 14 (top);
    Open Best Design Stock: p. 9 (bottom); Dmitry
    Pichugin: p. 14 (bottom); Bill Ragan: p. 17
    (bottom); Sculpies: p. 25 (top); Jarno Gonzalez
    Zarraonandia: p. 5, 13; P. Zonzel: front cover
Topham: p. 10 (center)

Illustrations:
Geoff Ward: p. 18 (center)

Series created by Brown Reference Group

Brown Reference Group have made every attempt to
contact the copyright holders of all pictures used in this
work. Please contact info@brownreference.com if you
have any information identifying copyright ownership.

Library and Archives Canada Cataloguing in Publication

Hyde, Natalie, 1963-
    History mysteries revealed / Natalie Hyde.

(Mysteries revealed)
Includes index.
ISBN 978-0-7787-7414-3 (bound).--ISBN 978-0-7787-7429-7 (pbk.)

    1. Civilization, Ancient--Juvenile literature.
2. World history--Juvenile literature. I. Title.

D21.3.H93 2010   j909   C2009-906261-5

Library of Congress Cataloging-in-Publication Data

Hyde, Natalie, 1963-
 History mysteries revealed / Natalie Hyde.
    p. cm. -- (Mysteries revealed)
 Includes index.
 ISBN 978-0-7787-7429-7 (pbk. : alk. paper)
 -- ISBN 978-0-7787-7414-3 (reinforced library binding : alk. paper)
 1. World history--Juvenile literature. 2. Civilization, Ancient--
Juvenile literature. 3. Curiosities and wonders--Juvenile
literature. I. Title. II. Series.

D21.3.H93 2010
909--dc22
                                                    2009042769

Crabtree Publishing Company

www.crabtreebooks.com   1-800-387-7650

Printed in the U.S.A./122009/BG20091103

Published in Canada
Crabtree Publishing
616 Welland Ave.
St. Catharines, Ontario
L2M 5V6

Published in the United States
Crabtree Publishing
PMB 59051
350 Fifth Avenue, 59th Floor
New York, New York 10118

Contents

Introduction   **4**

How did humans first reach America?   **6**

Where were the first cities?   8

How did Easter Islanders choose their leaders?   9

Were Neanderthals very different from modern people?   10

How did people find food before farming?   11

Why was the Great Wall of China built?   **12**

When did the Mongol Hordes rule Asia?   14

How did samurai warriors fight?   15

Where did the Silk Road go?   16

Who were the Boat People?   17

When did the first ship sail around the world?   **18**

How did feudalism work?   20

What was so great about Alexander the Great?   21

Did Vikings wear horns on their helmets?   22

Where was No Man's Land during World War I?   23

What was found inside the Great Pyramid?   **24**

How did Spain conquer the Incas?   26

Why did the Blue People make pillars of salt?   27

Who built the Great Serpent Mound?   28

When was the first democracy started?   29

History Facts   **30**

Find Out More   **30**

Glossary   **31**

Index   **32**

Introduction

The past is a fascinating place, with treasure hunters finding lost cities, fierce battles fought using elephants, and ancient **engineers** building massive tombs and temples. However, a lot of history is still a mystery. Experts must piece together what we know to figure just how people lived in the past—and why.

If you were living thousands of years ago in one of the world's first cities, your life would be very different. There would be no grocery stores, no books to read, and children played with sticks and dried bones. However, your ancient city would not be totally different from a modern one. Water was supplied to many homes, and sewers took away the waste. You could take a swim at a public bath and then go to the theater—there was even graffiti on the walls!

Spreading ideas

Ancient civilizations kept coming up with new ways of life. These ideas were spread around the world along trade routes and by explorers. Some ideas caught on wherever they went, but many ancient ways of life were lost. Historians are still solving some of history's mysteries, such as why Vikings had horned helmets or what Egypt's pyramids were actually for.

AMAZING!

The Muisca people of Colombia made an unusual offering to their gods. They covered their chief in gold dust and watched him bathe in a **sacred** lake. This tradition led to the legend of El Dorado—a place where gold was everywhere.

engineers People who design and construct things

Machu Pichu in Peru was a hidden city. The place had been empty for 400 years when it was discovered in 1911.

sacred Important because it is linked to religion or the spirits

How did humans first reach America?

By about 30,000 years ago, humans had spread from Africa to Europe, Asia, and Australia. But there were still no Americans.

> **"What is the difference between exploring and being lost?"**
> **Dan Eldon**

No one is sure exactly when people reached America. The latest idea is that people traveled from Siberia in eastern Asia about 25,000 years ago. At that time, ice covered most of Alaska and Canada—only islands and narrow strips of coast were ice free. The first Americans traveled in boats down the West Coast around the ice. They then headed south over land, and even reached the Amazon rain forest. The **ancestors** of most of today's Native Americans began arriving about 17,000 years ago. At that time, Alaska and Siberia were joined by a bridge of land, so people could just walk across. By 9,000 years ago, the **land bridge** had disappeared under the sea.

The first Americans could have arrived in boats made from animal skin like the ones used by today's Inuit people.

ancestors The relatives who lived before you did

▼ The ancestors of today's Native Americans were not the first humans to reach America.

AMAZING!

The Yahgans lived in Tierra del Fuego, a group of islands at the southern tip of South America. The Yahgans traveled between islands in canoes, but only the women could swim. The men never learned how to.

land bridge A strip of dry land that runs through the sea, linking two places

◀ Damascus in Syria is one of the oldest cities in the world. People have lived there for thousands of years.

Where were the first cities?

The first cities were in **Mesopotamia**. This is a strip of land in Iraq, lying between the Tigris and Euphrates rivers. The early cities were built about 7,500 years ago by the Sumerians. They invented a system of writing to keep city records. The *Epic of Gilgamesh*, the oldest story known, was written by a Sumerian.

AMAZING!

At the heart of the Sahara Desert are rock carvings of buffalo, gazelles, and even fish. This puzzled scientists. The nearest river is thousands of miles away. Researchers believe the desert was once a vast grassland that had rivers running through it.

◀ Sumerian writing is called cuneiform. Words were written in wet clay using a pen, or stylus, made of a reed.

Mesopotamia The name for an ancient region in the Middle East

How did Easter Islanders choose their leaders?

Easter Island is a remote island in the Pacific Ocean. The island was ruled by Tangatu Manu, the Birdman. Each year, a new leader was chosen from the island's most important men. Each **candidate** appointed a strong athlete as their champion, or hopu. The hopus raced down a steep cliff into the ocean and swam through shark-infested waters to a small, rocky island. The hopus then had to find an egg of a sooty tern nesting there, swim back across the water, and climb the cliff. The first candidate to receive an egg from his hopu was crowned as the Birdman for the year.

🔺 Hopus swam to Motu Nui, the third island from the cliffs. Many hopus died during the race.

HISTORY EXPLAINED

Easter Island has many huge and mysterious statues carved out of stone. They have oversized heads with long noses and ears, small bodies, and no legs. The tallest is more than 33 feet (10 m) high. The statues are thought to show the faces of important dead rulers and were sacred to ancient islanders.

candidate A person in line for a job

Were Neanderthals very different from modern people?

◗ Neanderthals are named for a valley in Germany where the first bones were found.

Neanderthals are sometimes called "cave men." They lived in Europe and the Middle East about 100,000 years ago. Neanderthals were very close relatives of us, modern humans, but they were not our direct ancestors. Scientists can tell from ancient skeletons that Neanderthals were stronger than modern humans. They had wider shoulders and thicker bones. They also had a bulging ridge running above their eyes. Tough bodies helped the Neanderthals survive the cold of the **Ice Age**. However, when the world began to warm up again, modern humans arrived from Africa and began to take over. The last Neanderthals died out about 28,000 years ago.

Neanderthals had larger brains than us, but were they as clever? ◗

Ice Age A time when Earth was colder and had ice covering large areas

How did people find food before farming?

Before people learned to grow food and keep animals, they found their food. We call these people hunter-gatherers. They gathered things such as fruits, nuts, roots, and eggs, but to get meat they had to trap or hunt wild animals. Experts used to think that the men were hunters and the women did the gathering. However, it is likely that the best hunters—both men and women—went on trips together.

🔺 Some people live as hunter-gatherers even today. This boy from the Amazon has caught a wild animal.

HISTORY EXPLAINED

Humans eat grass! Bread, cookies, and pastries—anything made from regular flour—is mainly powdered grass seeds, or grains. The first grains were collected from wild grasses. People began to farm wheat in Turkey about 10,000 years ago. Wild grass shatters, or drops its grains, making it difficult to collect them. The first farmers chose plants that held on to their seeds. Over the **centuries**, farmers bred better wheat, barley, and other grain crops, making them taller and tastier than wild plants.

We eat only the seeds of wheat; the stalks are known as straw. ◗

Why was the Great Wall of China built?

About 2,300 years ago, seven small countries joined together to become the first Chinese **empire**. It had many enemies, and there were many forts and walls to defend against them. China's emperor decided to join them together— and began the largest construction project in history.

It took nearly 2,000 years to complete the wall. Slaves, prisoners, and soldiers did most of the work. By the 1600s, the Great Wall of China ran for 4,500 miles (7,242 km) through the north of the country. Much of it is built in steep mountains, making the construction very dangerous work. So many people died building the wall that it is called the longest **cemetery** on Earth.

"Life ends, while knowledge goes on forever."
Zhuang Zi

At one time, the ◗ Great Wall was guarded by one million soldiers.

cemetery A place where dead people are buried

empire A large area, often containing several countries, that is ruled by an emperor

When did the Mongol Hordes rule Asia?

The Mongol Empire was the largest empire that has ever existed. It was started by a man called Temujin, who was the khan, or chief, of several families. He began to take control of neighboring families, and in the year 1206 he took the name Genghis Khan, which means Universal Ruler. He brought peace to Mongolia and organized his people into a powerful nation. Genghis Khan then began invading his neighbors. His huge army of fierce and highly skilled warriors became known as the Mongol Horde. The soldiers' families followed the army, so the Mongols fought battles far from home. By 1294, the Mongol Empire covered one fifth of Earth's land. It stretched from Eastern Europe to the China Sea and from Siberia to the Persian Gulf.

⬆ **Mongolian soldiers dressed in traditional uniforms.**

◀ **The grassland of Mongolia is the home of the horse, and the Mongol army fought on horseback.**

martial arts Fighting systems mostly coming from East Asia

How did samurai warriors fight?

The samurai were masters of **martial arts** in Japan. They worked as soldiers or policemen for the emperor or other masters. The way a samurai lived, fought—and even died—was set out by rules called the *Bushido*. *Bushido* means "the way of the warrior." A samurai was expected to be very loyal and brave enough to die for his master. But he also had to be calm and fair. If a samurai broke one of the rules, or was beaten in battle, he was expected to take his own life.

◁ Samurai warriors fought with swords and bows and wore armor made from metal plates and leather.

AMAZING!

Archaeologists are puzzled about **mummies** found in a desert in Asia. These 3,000-year-old mummies do not look like ancestors of today's Chinese people. They have red-blonde hair and fair skin. Scientists think northern Europeans traveled into Asia and settled there.

Where did the Silk Road go?

The Silk Road was not one road but a series of trade routes. They went all the way from China to the Mediterranean Sea. Merchants in the west traded gold and silver for silk, spices, and fine porcelain—or china—from the east. People rarely traveled along the whole route. They would cross one section and sell their goods to the next merchant. Their journeys were still long and dangerous. The route crossed the Taklamakan Desert in Central Asia and passed through the Karakoram Mountains in Pakistan. Cities grew up along the Silk Road as trade centers.

⬤ In the days of the Silk Road, no one in Europe knew how to make silk, so they had to buy it from China.

⬤ Khiva in Uzbekistan was once a bustling merchant city on the Silk Road.

refugees People who run away from wars, diseases, or bad living conditions

Who were the Boat People?

Boat People are **refugees** who are forced to leave their country by making dangerous sea journeys. The biggest group of Boat People were from Vietnam. After the Vietnam War ended in 1975, one million people decided to leave. Over the next ten years, people sailed small ships out into the South China Sea. People on the ships were often robbed by pirates and many of the crowded boats sank in storms. The lucky ones reached Hong Kong or Taiwan. Many of them were then given a place to live in the United States and Canada.

Boat People arrived with almost nothing.

HISTORY EXPLAINED

△ **More than two million Americans served in Vietnam in the 1960s and 1970s.**

Vietnam used to be run by France. In World War II, the Japanese took over. When they left in 1945, a **communist** group called the Viet Minh said they were in charge. However, France disagreed, and a war began. In 1954, the French were defeated, and it was decided that Vietnam would become two countries. South Vietnam was friendly with the United States, while North Vietnam was communist and supported by Russia, which was an enemy of America at the time. By 1960 the two Vietnams were at war, and American troops were sent to help South Vietnam fight the communists. However, U.S. forces could not stop South Vietnam from becoming communist in 1975.

When did the first ship sail around the world?

Ferdinand Magellan left Spain in 1519 and sailed west. He was looking for a new way to get to Asia—in the east!

After crossing the Atlantic Ocean, Magellan sailed down the coast of South America. Eventually, he found a way into the Pacific Ocean. His three ships sailed non-stop for nearly four months across the Pacific, with little fresh water and only maggot-infested biscuits to eat. Many of the crew died from hunger and disease. At last, Magellan reached the Philippines, but he was soon killed in a battle with islanders. Just one ship, the *Victoria*, continued on around Africa and back to Spain. Of the 234 men who had set out, only 18 returned home.

⬢ **Magellan's expedition** to circle the world took three years to complete.

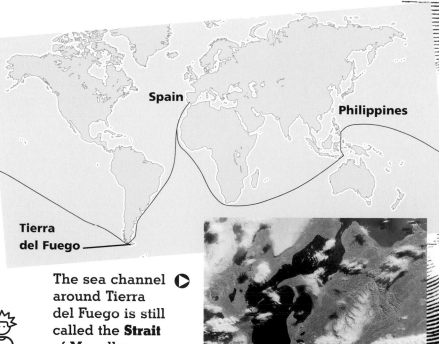

Spain

Philippines

Tierra del Fuego

⬤ The sea channel around Tierra del Fuego is still called the **Strait** of Magellan.

expedition A journey or voyage taken for a specific purpose

◀ Ferdinand Magellan was the first European to sail across the Pacific Ocean.

AMAZING!

The Lenox Globe in the New York Public Library is one of the oldest globes in the world. Experts think it was made even before Magellan's voyage. It is constructed of copper and on the east coast of Asia it warns: "Here be dragons."

strait A narrow channel of sea that passes between land areas

How did feudalism work?

Feudalism was the way Europe was governed until only a few centuries ago. The king (or queen) owned all the land and gave sections of it to barons. In return, the baron provided an army when the king needed it. The barons divided their land among their knights, who would lead troops in battle. The knights rented land to farmers called yeomen, who would also fight alongside their master in times of war. All the work was done by people called serfs. Under the system, serfs did not have to fight for their lord—but were often forced to anyway.

⚠ Knights could afford armor and good weapons, but most foot soldiers had only a sharpened stick or a farm tool, such as a pitchfork.

AMAZING!

No one knows if King Arthur was real. Most of the stories about him are legend, but there are old documents about Arthur Pendragon. Pendragon was a Welsh hero who defended the country from Danish invaders 1,200 years ago.

Cleopatra A queen who ruled Egypt about 2,000 years ago

What was so great about Alexander the Great?

Alexander was only 20 years old when he became king of Macedon in Greece. Nevertheless, Alexander was a skilled military leader who was able to defeat armies much larger than his own. In fact, he never lost a battle. He conquered Egypt and **Persia** and combined them into a strong empire that stretched all the way to India. In Europe, Alexander is seen as a mighty conqueror, but in Asia he is remembered as Iskander the Terrible, a devilish invader.

Alexander the Great died at the age of 32, probably from malaria. ▶

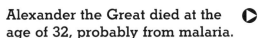

⚠ The Pharo fell down in an earthquake in the 1300s.

HISTORY EXPLAINED

Alexander the Great founded many cities across his empire—and named them all after himself. The most famous is Alexandria, which was the capital of Egypt for 1,000 years. It was home to Queen **Cleopatra**. It had the largest library in the ancient world and was famous for its lighthouse, or Pharo. This was built in the 3rd century B.C. and stood about 400 feet (122 m) tall.

Did Vikings wear horns on their helmets?

Roman and Greek writers were the first to report that people in northern Europe wore horns on their helmets in battle. **Archaeologists** have found no proof of this. They know that **Norse**, or Viking, people wore horned headgear during ceremonies. But the helmets we have found have no horns at all.

◀ A historian dresses up as a Viking to find out more about how they lived.

HISTORY EXPLAINED

Leif Eriksson was a Viking explorer who lived in Greenland in the 1000s. He had heard rumors about land even farther to the west and wanted to explore it. He sailed with a crew of 35 (right) and landed in what is now L'Anse aux Meadows on the northern tip of Newfoundland, Canada. Archaeologists have found what is left of the Viking's American home. It had eight buildings with iron works and a yard for repairing ships. No one knows how long the Vikings lived in America. Cloak pins, knitting needles, and spindles found there suggest that women and children might have lived there, too.

archaeologists Scientists who study the things left behind by ancient people

Where was No Man's Land during World War I?

⬤ The first tanks were used in 1916 and helped troops to cross No Man's Land.

In 1914, Europe was split in two by the largest war the world had seen. France, Britain, Italy, and Russia were fighting Germany, Austria, and the Turkish empire. Much of the fighting was in France and Belgium. Soldiers moved on foot, tanks had not been invented, and no side had an advantage over the other. The giant armies soon reached stalemate— no one was winning, but no one was losing either. The soldiers dug defensive trenches a short distance from the enemy, and waited for orders. The empty space between the two lines became known as No Man's Land. It took four years of fighting and ten million dead soldiers before France and Britain finally won.

Norse The name for ancient people from Scandinavia, including the Vikings

What was found inside the Great Pyramid?

The Great Pyramid of Giza is one of the Seven Ancient Wonders of the World. Archaeologists think it was built as a tomb for the pharaoh called Khufu.

> **"History never looks like history when you are living through it."**
> **John W. Gardner**

In 1820 A.D., workmen broke through the outer wall of the pyramid and found a passage leading to a large room—now named the King's Chamber. Other Egyptian tombs were full of games, furniture, and jewelry, but this one was empty. The only thing in it was a **granite** box with no lid. Some thought it was a sarcophagus, or stone coffin, but it was too short for even a medium-sized mummy. A smaller chamber, called the Queen's Chamber was also empty. There may be more hidden tunnels and rooms in the pyramid yet to be discovered.

The only way into the Great Pyramid is through a tunnel dug through the rock.

granite A hard rock made inside mountains

The pyramids at Giza, Egypt, were originally covered in flat stones. Only the middle one has any left.

AMAZING!

Some researchers have suggested that the flat limestone blocks used to cover the pyramids were not carved from rocks but were made from special concrete.

pharaoh A king of ancient Egypt

How did Spain conquer the Incas?

A Spanish explorer, or **conquistador**, named Francisco Pizarro went to South America looking for treasure. His army had just 180 soldiers. In 1531, they arrived in Peru, the heart of the Inca empire. To the Incas, gold was so common that it was not thought to be valuable. Pizarro invited the Inca leader, Atahualpa, to meet him. The Spanish tricked the Incas and killed Atahualpa. The Inca army retreated when their leader was murdered. The tiny Spanish force captured Cuzco, the Inca capital, in 1533. The Incas had never seen horses and were easily beaten by the Spanish cannons.

Atahualpa offered Pizarro one room full of gold and two of silver if he would let him go. Atahualpa gave him the treasure, but Pizarro still murdered him.

conquistador A Spanish conqueror who went to America to find gold and treasure

A Tuareg's thin, blue ◗ headscarf keeps his head cool and shields his face in sandstorms.

Why did the Blue People make pillars of salt?

The Tuareg are traders in the Sahara Desert. The men wear headscarves made of dyed blue cloth and this is how they get the name "Blue People." The Tuareg have been trading salt for centuries, carrying it across the desert from Niger to Morocco. The salt comes from shallow ponds near Bilma, Niger. The pond water evaporates in the heat leaving crusts of salt behind. The soggy white salt crystals are pressed on to cone-shaped molds and left to harden into pillars. The pillars are a good shape for strapping to a camel. Farmers buy the pillars as **salt licks** for their animals.

AMAZING!

Few people realize it, but Timbuktu is a real place. It is in Mali, on the southern edge of the Sahara Desert. Today it is a quiet sandy city, but about 700 years ago, Timbuktu was the main trading post in West Africa. Gold, salt, ivory, and slaves were all sold at its busy markets.

salt licks Blocks of salt used in hot countries to keep animals healthy

Who built the Great Serpent Mound?

⬭ The serpent mound is 1,330 feet (405 m) long.

The Great Serpent Mound in Ohio is a mound of earth in the shape of a snake. It is the largest earthwork of its kind in the world. Scientists cannot agree on who built the mound and when. Some believe it was the Adena people. Two Adena burial mounds were found next to the serpent. Other researchers believe the Fort Ancients built the mound 1,000 years ago. This group built other mounds in the shapes of other creatures. We are still working to solve this mystery.

AMAZING!

The Beehive Chambers in Greece are domed rooms made of interlocking stones. The stones fit so perfectly that no mortar was used. Archaeologists think they may have been ancient tombs.

treasurer A person in charge of money

When was the first democracy started?

The city of Athens, Greece, was a democracy 2,500 years ago. Citizens did not elect leaders as we do today. They voted on all the laws themselves. The only people who had the right to vote were citizens of Athens. They also had to be adult males who had completed their military training. Each citizen would also have to take his turn in charge. They were not elected but were given certain positions through a lottery. Only the city **treasurer** and military generals were elected. These positions needed men who were most experienced.

○ Citizens gathered on a hill in Athens to discuss problems.

○ Socrates often sat in Athens' marketplace and argued with people.

HISTORY EXPLAINED

Socrates was a **philosopher** in ancient Athens. He did not think democracy was the best way to rule the city. He did not believe that people without a good education were the best people to lead or make important decisions. He believed that a government should only be run by philosophers. Experts would be appointed to advise them. Socrates was not afraid to spread his ideas, but many people thought they were dangerous. The citizens sentenced him to death! In Athens, criminals had to kill themselves by drinking a poison called hemlock.

philosopher A person who tries to answer questions that science cannot explain

History Facts

Hannibal was a general from Carthage, Tunisia. He marched his army, including war elephants, through the Alps to invade Italy.

The Colosseum in Rome could be flooded with water for mock sea battles.

King Nebuchadnezzar of Babylon had a Persian wife. She was homesick for the lush gardens of her homeland. To please her, the king built terraces shaped like mountains and covered them with plants. They became the Hanging Gardens of Babylon.

Find Out More

Books

The World Almanac for Kids Puzzler Deck World History & Geography! by Lynn Brunelle. Chronicle Books, 2007.

Calliope, World History Magazine for Kids, Carus Publishing.

The Horrible History of the World by Terry Deary. Scholastic, 2007.

Web sites

History and Science for Kids
www.historyforkids.org

Tudor England Joust game
www.tudorbritain.org/joust/index.asp

National Geographic history
www.nationalgeographic.com/history

Glossary

ancestors The relatives who lived before you did

archaeologists Scientists who study the things left behind by ancient people

candidate A person in line for a job

cemetery A place where dead people are buried

centuries Periods of time that contain 100 years

Cleopatra A queen who ruled Egypt about 2,000 years ago

communist A person who wants to live in a country were everything is shared

conquistador A Spanish conqueror who went to America to find gold and treasure

empire A large area, often containing several countries, that is ruled by an emperor

engineers People who design and construct things

expedition A journey or voyage taken for a specific purpose

granite A hard rock made inside mountains

Ice Age A time when Earth was colder and had ice covering large areas

land bridge A strip of dry land that runs through the sea linking two places

martial arts Fighting systems mostly coming from East Asia

Mesopotamia The name for an ancient region in the Middle East

mummies The remains of dead bodies that have survived hundreds or thousands of years

Norse The name for ancient people from Scandinavia, including the Vikings

Persia An old name for Iran and the surrounding area; Persia was once a huge empire

pharaoh A king of ancient Egypt

philosopher A person who tries to answer questions that science cannot explain

refugees People who run away from wars, diseases, or bad living conditions

sacred Important because it is linked to religion or the spirits

salt licks Blocks of salt used in hot countries to keep animals healthy

strait A narrow channel of sea that passes between land areas

treasurer A person in charge of money

Index

Africa 6, 10, 18, 27
Alexander the Great 21
  Alexandria 21
  Cleopatra 21
archaeologists 15, 22, 24, 28
Asia 6, 14, 15, 16, 18, 19, 21
Athens, Greece 29
Australia 6
Canada 6, 17, 22
China 12–13, 16, 17
Colosseum 30
conquistador 26
Damascus 8
Easter Island 9
Egypt 4, 21, 24–25
  Great Pyramid 24
El Dorado 4
Eriksson, Leif 22
Europe 6, 10, 14, 16, 20, 21, 22, 23
farming 11, 20, 27
Genghis Khan 14
Great Serpent Mound 28
Great Wall of China 12
Hanging Gardens of Babylon 30
Ice Age 10
Incas 26
King Arthur 20

knights 20
land bridge 6
Magellan, Ferdinand 18–19
Mediterranean Sea 16
Mesopotamia 8
Mongol Empire 14
Native Americans 6–7
  Inuit 6
  Yahgans 7
Neanderthals 10
No Man's Land 23
Pacific Ocean 9, 18, 19
Peru 5, 26
pyramids 4, 24–25
refugees 17
Sahara Desert 8, 27
Siberia 6, 14
Silk Road 16
South America 7, 18, 26
Sumeria 8
Tierra del Fuego 7, 18
Timbuktu 27
tombs 4, 24, 28
United States 17
Vietnam War 17
Vikings 4, 22
World War I 23